MW01590967

The
Quest of the Four Chiefs
for the
Book of Heaven

ISBN 979-8-89428-065-3 (paperback)
ISBN 979-8-89428-066-0 (hardcover)
ISBN 979-8-89428-067-7 (digital)

Copyright © 2024 by Kyle St. Penney

All rights reserved. No part of this publication may be reproduced, distributed, or transmitted in any form or by any means, including photocopying, recording, or other electronic or mechanical methods without the prior written permission of the publisher. For permission requests, solicit the publisher via the address below.

Christian Faith Publishing
832 Park Avenue
Meadville, PA 16335
www.christianfaithpublishing.com

Printed in the United States of America

The
Quest of the Four Chiefs
for the
Book of Heaven

Kyle St. Penney

A long time ago, during the time of cowboys and indigenous people in the western home of the setting sun lands, there was a great council of tribes. The Mountain Tribe, the Plains Tribe, and even the Rolling Hills Tribe gathered at this council of leaders. These leaders were called chiefs, who led their tribes with wisdom, honor, respect, sacrifice, and especially love.

They gathered together because these tribes had met those whom they called the white men, who usually were cowboys. But they were not scared of the white man. They met together because the white man had knowledge he hadn't shared with the tribes yet.

One chief told the other chiefs that he had a dream from the Great Spirit that the white man had words from the Great Spirit. This chief had these words of the Great Spirit himself, written down in his own language. Then another chief spoke too about how another white man spoke to his tribe about these words and how the tribe gathered so close to hear what this white man had to say.

The chief had said that the white man told the people of the tribe that these words are written for every man and woman, not just the white man. He told them that the words tell how the Great Spirit wants to be worshipped. The council of chiefs settled that they would send for these words, words written down in what the council now called the Book of Heaven. Four chiefs were sent, two from the Nez Perce and two from the Flathead tribes, to bring teachers of the Book of Heaven that their people would read them too.

And so, from Idaho, these four chiefs made the journey from the setting sun lands to the rising sun lands. Across plains, through the trees, they climbed mountains, swam rivers, hiked canyons, and walked through deserts to finally reach the Mississippi River's edge: St. Louis. Because the Nez Perce knew Lewis and Clark nearly thirty years prior, the chiefs went to the government office of General William Clarke.

But because the chiefs only knew of the white man and not his language, William Clark did not speak their language, and Sacajawea was no longer with Lewis and Clark. So the white man whom the chiefs journeyed to see could not understand what they were saying when they asked about the Book of Heaven. The chiefs really wanted the words of the Great Spirit for their people, so they only got excited and angry because they did not want to return home without these words.

But someone else wanted the Book of Heaven shared with the people of the four chiefs: the Great *Spirit* Himself. Many people call fortune as luck or fate, but even the indigenous tribes know that all days and all the lands belong to the Great Spirit. And the Great Spirit guided the spirit of another chief to the office of General Clarke; his name was William Walker Jr.

Back in the days of the Wild West, many tribes moved their homes across the land, hunted and gathered where they could, and even traded with different tribes. And because these tribes spoke different languages, they used a common sign language to help them communicate. The four chiefs and Chief William Walker Jr. knew this sign language. He was the interpreter for them to General Clarke.

And General Clarke told the four chiefs the words of the Great Spirit, the *Holy Spirit*, and all things the Book of Heaven tells about *King Jesus the Messiah*. These four chiefs received their Creator's gift of life; they placed trust in *King Jesus the Messiah*. But they could not just stay the same; they had to share their faith with their people and the Book of Heaven in their words. They needed a teacher of the Book of Heaven.

But two of the chiefs fell sick, and the Great Spirit called two of the chiefs back home into the spirit world. Their bones were buried in St. Louis and their spirits sent to *King Jesus* himself. So the two chiefs had to return home.

The interpreter could not go with them because he had his own family, but he did do a great act for them. Because this was long before the Internet, the newspaper was the next best thing, and William Walker wrote a letter to the newspaper about the two Nez Perce and two Flathead chiefs coming to St. Louis in search of the Book of Heaven in their words.

13

The newspaper told missionaries who were willing to go to the Rocky Mountains, to teach the tribes the blessed words of the Book of Heaven. Not many answered the call from the newspaper, but the two missionaries who did come to Idaho, they were met with crowds of Nez Perce people, who gave their warmest welcome party.

And one missionary learned the language of the Nez Perce tribe. He then translated the book of Matthew into their language. Not every Nez Perce placed their faith in who some called the white man's God, but one Nez Perce man did. He even took a name from the Book of Heaven as his new name, Joseph. And he became who we all know as Chief Joseph.

About the Author

Kyle Stuart Penney was born in May 1989, in Lewiston, Idaho, and is an enrolled member of the Nez Perce tribe. He grew up in various places, including Kamiah, Idaho, and Bellingham, Washington. After facing personal challenges and changes in residence, he eventually settled near Boise in the Treasure Valley.

Kyle met his wife, Abbagail, in late 2019. They began dating after Easter, he proposed by Thanksgiving, and they were married by Christmas of 2020. They welcomed their son, Asher, in June 2022, followed by their daughter, Aviela, in August 2023.

Printed in the USA
CPSIA information can be obtained
at www.ICGtesting.com
CBHW062044111024
15568CB00071B/145